Student Word Lists, Passages, and Early Literacy Assessments

Basic Reading Inventory

Tenth Edition

Jerry L. Johns

KENDALL/HUNT PUBLISHING COMPANY

4050 Westmark Drive   Dubuque, Iowa 52002

www.kendallhunt.com/readingresources

Contents

Form

Graded Word Lists

List AA	**List A**
1. me	1. show
2. get	2. play
3. home	3. be
4. not	4. eat
5. he	5. did
6. tree	6. brown
7. girl	7. is
8. take	8. boat
9. book	9. call
10. milk	10. run
11. dog	11. what
12. all	12. him
13. apple	13. wagon
14. like	14. over
15. go	15. but
16. farm	16. on
17. went	17. had
18. friend	18. this
19. about	19. around
20. some	20. sleep

List A 7141

1. here
2. down
3. then
4. how
5. saw
6. pocket
7. hello
8. aunt
9. never
10. puppy
11. could
12. after
13. hill
14. men
15. gone
16. ran
17. gave
18. or
19. way
20. coat

List A 8224

1. ten
2. poor
3. city
4. teacher
5. turn
6. fight
7. because
8. soft
9. open
10. winter
11. joke
12. different
13. say
14. quiet
15. sister
16. above
17. seed
18. thought
19. such
20. chase

List A 3183

1. trail
2. stream
3. beach
4. snake
5. lift
6. cabin
7. bless
8. rooster
9. journey
10. treasure
11. hero
12. beyond
13. moan
14. glitter
15. impossible
16. shot
17. island
18. manage
19. receive
20. automobile

List A 5414

1. stove
2. government
3. program
4. grape
5. favorite
6. blizzard
7. noon
8. greet
9. sport
10. rumble
11. tropical
12. language
13. expert
14. nervous
15. starve
16. voyage
17. silence
18. scamper
19. prairie
20. moccasin

COPY

List A 8595

1. lizard
2. double
3. scarlet
4. helmet
5. dusk
6. bandit
7. loyal
8. choice
9. furnish
10. century
11. kindergarten
12. entrance
13. dentist
14. celebration
15. blister
16. symbol
17. drowsy
18. attach
19. rehearse
20. terrace

List A 6867

1. bleed
2. accomplishment
3. whimper
4. marriage
5. frisky
6. seam
7. backward
8. location
9. nightmare
10. gently
11. employ
12. broadcast
13. kennel
14. pulp
15. satisfaction
16. cushion
17. graduate
18. harmonica
19. definite
20. yacht

List A 3717

1. dwell
2. slogan
3. knapsack
4. administration
5. gangster
6. flatter
7. incredible
8. algebra
9. bachelor
10. vocabulary
11. longitude
12. saliva
13. peninsula
14. monarch
15. feminine
16. quench
17. competition
18. pollute
19. ambitious
20. orchid

List A 8183

1. quote
2. ventilate
3. surgeon
4. analyze
5. masterpiece
6. disinfectant
7. extraordinary
8. camouflage
9. ruthless
10. perpendicular
11. juvenile
12. vacancy
13. dictator
14. negative
15. honorary
16. custody
17. maneuver
18. faculty
19. pneumonia
20. embassy

List A 4959

1. random
2. disrupt
3. autobiography
4. expire
5. contestant
6. strategy
7. crave
8. detach
9. apprehend
10. idolize
11. consecutive
12. vacate
13. debatable
14. combustion
15. famished
16. detract
17. crochet
18. insomnia
19. siesta
20. bayonet

List A 1047

1. displacement
2. heritage
3. exponent
4. variable
5. preliminary
6. embryo
7. sterile
8. gratify
9. maternity
10. incorporate
11. gore
12. illogical
13. radiate
14. forum
15. predominant
16. fictitious
17. cuticle
18. panorama
19. inquisitive
20. artisan

List A 1187

1. insensible

2. beneficiary

3. spectrum

4. idealism

5. epic

6. composite

7. informant

8. ransack

9. interlude

10. suede

11. renaissance

12. dissociate

13. commemorate

14. populous

15. fraudulent

16. inquisition

17. dexterity

18. lenient

19. dilapidated

20. disheveled

List A 1296

1. denote

2. hallowed

3. transcend

4. affiliate

5. obtuse

6. recipient

7. consensus

8. concentric

9. postulate

10. impel

11. collateral

12. repugnant

13. promissory

14. meticulous

15. flippant

16. sardonic

17. indemnity

18. adamant

19. effigy

20. tithe

Form A

Graded Passages

A Green Frog

A green frog sits on a rock.

It has big back legs.

It can jump up.

It can swim in the pond.

It gets wet.

Walk in the Fall

It was fall. Pat went for a walk. She took her dog Sam. They liked to walk. They walked for a long time. They saw trees. Some were red. Some were green. They were pretty. Pat and Sam saw birds too. Sam did not run after them. He was nice.

The First Snow

Jack woke up Saturday morning. He looked out of the window. The ground was white. The trees were white.

"Oh boy," said Jack, "snow."

"What did you say?" asked Tom, opening his eyes.

"It snowed last night. Get up and see," said Jack.

Both boys ran to the window.

"Look at that!" said Tom. "Come on. Let's get dressed."

Jack and Tom ran into the kitchen.

"Mom!" they said. "It snowed last night."

"Yes," said Mom. "Dad went out to get your sleds. First we will eat breakfast. Then we can have some fun. The first snow is the best!"

Spotty Swims

One day Spotty went for a walk. The sun was warm. Spotty walked to the pond. There he saw a frog. The frog was on a log. Spotty wanted to play. Spotty began to bark. The frog jumped into the water.

Then Spotty jumped into the water. But poor Spotty did not know what to do. The water was very deep. The water went way over his head. Spotty moved his legs. Soon his head came out of the water. He kept on moving. He came to the other side of the pond. That is how Spotty learned to swim.

Bill at Camp

It was the first time Bill went to camp. He was very happy to be there. Soon he went for a walk in the woods to look for many kinds of leaves. He found leaves from some maple and oak trees. As Bill walked in the woods, he saw some animal tracks. At that moment, a mouse ran into a small hole by a tree. Bill wondered if the tracks were made by the mouse. He looked around for other animals. He did not see any. The last thing Bill saw was an old bird nest in a pine tree.

The Hungry Bear

The busy bees had been making honey all day. That night it was cool and damp. I had slept well until I heard a loud noise near my window. It sounded as if someone were trying to break into my cabin. As I moved from my cot, I could see something black standing near the window. In fright I knocked on the window. Very slowly and quietly the great shadow moved back and went away. The next day we found huge bear tracks. The bear had come for the honey the bees were making in the attic of the cabin.

Fire and Animals

The summer was a dry one, unusual
for this area. Trees and bushes in the forest
wilted and died. One afternoon a storm
came to the forest. Thunder was heard and
lightning was seen. Then it began to
rain. A spark touched the leaves and a
fire began. The fire spread quickly. The
animals warned each other as they hurried
to escape the flames. As the fire came
closer, trees fell to the ground. Their
branches were yellow, orange, and red.
The smoke was so thick that the animals
could hardly breathe. Many couldn't
escape the danger of the flames.

The Mystery

Everyone turned to stare as a black hooded figure whizzed by on a skateboard. It was a mystery because no one knew who the talented person was. Ken saw the skateboarder slide down the library railing and disappear into the alley. Nita followed the person from school and watched as a curb was jumped and a three hundred sixty degree turn was completed with ease. One day Ken noticed a skateboard and a black hooded jacket next to Rose's house. He also saw a library book called *Skateboarding Tips* in her desk at school. Ken had solved the challenging mystery.

Keep Your Distance

Elwood was considered a tough guy at Anderson School. Everybody called him Sky. They didn't dare call him by his full name because that riled him. He was colossal in size. From far away Elwood looked like Mr. Wilson, a teacher, but the moment you saw Elwood's shoes and faded, torn jeans, you knew it could only be Elwood. He felt inferior because of his clothing, so he tried to make up for it by shocking people with his rude behavior and toughness. Elwood didn't have many friends, except for Bob who lived in the same old brick apartment building.

Looming Danger

The foreheads of the soldiers glistened with sweat as they struggled forward under the blazing sun of the tropics. This small band of soldiers sincerely felt that their leader was the salvation of their country. Their objective was to reach a distant army fort where they hoped to fire a rocket into the storeroom of the fort. This would cause the gunpowder to erupt like a tinderbox. A huge person bellowed an order from the leader as they trudged across the uninhabited land. The soldiers hoped their attack would scare enemy soldiers and impress more local people to join them.

A Scientist's Search

Chris, a scientist, worked hard at the lab bench. Chris had been given a very stimulating suggestion in a letter from an unknown person. The key to success was in the radium reaction that would activate the needed medicine. From that point, it was simply a matter of reducing different compounds to find the right one. Ultimately, it would be found, and then Chris would have a monopoly on the medicine that could make people immortal. Only Chris would know the correct amount in each tablet. The disappearance of death and disease would make Chris the most powerful person alive.

Form  B

Graded Word Lists

List BB	**List B**
1. we	1. they
2. and	2. she
3. house	3. will
4. the	4. of
5. duck	5. blue
6. one	6. it
7. street	7. are
8. happy	8. his
9. lost	9. now
10. first	10. dress
11. do	11. if
12. at	12. from
13. very	13. morning
14. find	14. father
15. out	15. ask
16. party	16. back
17. goat	17. green
18. wish	18. time
19. know	19. who
20. sing	20. cookie

List B 7141

1. little
2. next
3. reads
4. my
5. make
6. old
7. mother
8. bed
9. grow
10. laugh
11. near
12. before
13. lamb
14. ride
15. store
16. high
17. began
18. made
19. cry
20. her

List B 8224

1. feel
2. drink
3. wave
4. gray
5. start
6. horn
7. across
8. warm
9. bad
10. even
11. feed
12. always
13. round
14. country
15. enough
16. able
17. should
18. bottom
19. crawl
20. machine

COPY

List B 3183

1. star
2. net
3. doctor
4. spoon
5. trap
6. valley
7. shirt
8. meet
9. chuckle
10. gaze
11. rib
12. discover
13. hundred
14. reason
15. conductor
16. coast
17. escape
18. thirty
19. prepare
20. nation

List B 5414

1. bike
2. castle
3. jungle
4. bullet
5. factory
6. stripe
7. problem
8. target
9. capture
10. sleeve
11. pump
12. sausage
13. electric
14. business
15. instant
16. balance
17. surround
18. invention
19. accident
20. rifle

Form B • Graded Word Lists • Student Copy

List B 8595

1. science
2. blush
3. marvelous
4. index
5. panther
6. grace
7. boss
8. emergency
9. blond
10. nugget
11. terrific
12. effort
13. observe
14. mammoth
15. transportation
16. liberty
17. balcony
18. scar
19. confidence
20. admiral

List B 6867

1. painful
2. raspberry
3. medical
4. label
5. household
6. foreman
7. catalog
8. solar
9. unexpected
10. beggar
11. thermometer
12. portable
13. distrust
14. dandelion
15. charity
16. graduation
17. species
18. variety
19. contribute
20. jagged

List B 3717

1. focus
2. turnpike
3. harmony
4. uranium
5. merchandise
6. irregular
7. humidity
8. enlarge
9. expel
10. remainder
11. industrious
12. pamphlet
13. geologist
14. rayon
15. novel
16. survival
17. meteorite
18. dormitory
19. mahogany
20. chauffeur

List B 8183

1. skyscraper
2. reaction
3. horsepower
4. justify
5. garlic
6. omit
7. divorce
8. exception
9. flounder
10. comedian
11. nomination
12. barbarian
13. molecule
14. recruit
15. imperfect
16. upholster
17. authentic
18. variation
19. mortgage
20. brigade

List B 4959

1. disapprove
2. data
3. texture
4. disqualify
5. compress
6. slur
7. gruesome
8. deceased
9. transaction
10. misconduct
11. sarcasm
12. momentary
13. ingenious
14. mechanism
15. audible
16. embezzle
17. robust
18. luminous
19. heathen
20. ecstasy

List B 1047

1. immature
2. reorganize
3. evaluate
4. visualize
5. grim
6. patronize
7. rupture
8. chronic
9. exploit
10. obituary
11. saturate
12. induce
13. recuperate
14. pictorial
15. phenomenal
16. portal
17. centennial
18. silhouette
19. boisterous
20. impertinent

List B 1187

1. discredit
2. habitat
3. profane
4. intern
5. intimidate
6. inseparable
7. binder
8. bilingual
9. jurisdiction
10. stilt
11. metropolis
12. preposterous
13. pollinate
14. patronage
15. reminiscent
16. secede
17. knoll
18. promenade
19. catechism
20. cavalcade

List B 1296

1. invalidate
2. metabolism
3. metamorphosis
4. advert
5. impotent
6. predatory
7. protocol
8. prodigy
9. derivative
10. zealous
11. debase
12. pretentious
13. regurgitate
14. herbivorous
15. maritime
16. aesthetic
17. blasphemy
18. extemporaneous
19. agrarian
20. colloquial

COPY

Form

Graded Passages

The Pink Pig

The pink pig ran to the wet mud.

It was a big, fat pig.

The pig was hot.

It just sat in the wet mud.

Form B • Graded Passage • Student Copy

Birds

I can look for birds. I look up in a tree. I see a big bird. It is brown. I see a baby bird. It is little. It is brown too.

The big bird can fly. The baby bird can not fly. It is little. I like to see birds.

The Box

Ben went to see his friend Nan. He had a blue box. Nan saw the box. She said, "What is in the blue box?"

"I can not tell you," said Ben. Nan asked, "Is it a ball?"

"No, it is not a ball," said Ben. "Is it a car?" asked Nan.

"No, it is not a car," said Ben. "I know, it is an apple," said Nan.

Ben looked in the box. There were two apples. One apple was green. One apple was red. He gave the red apple to Nan. Nan liked the apple. Ben was a good friend.

Up a Tree

Jeff likes to play with his cat Boots. One day a dog walked by. Boots ran up a big tree.

Jeff said, "Come down Boots." The cat did not come down. Jeff did not know what to do. He called his mom.

His mom said, "Here Boots. Come here." The cat did not come.

Then Jeff went home. He came back with a bag. He put the bag down. He took out some milk. He walked to the tree with the milk. He said, "Here Boots. Come get some milk." Boots came down and had some milk. Jeff was happy.

The Strange Object

It was a breezy day in March. I was walking home thinking about my day at school. In the sky I saw a strange object. At first, I thought it was an airplane.

I climbed up a hill to get a better view. As I got closer, I saw it diving through the air in a strange way. It was brown and had wings. Maybe it was a bird.

Then the wind stopped, and the object came crashing toward me. I ran to get away. Then I heard a friendly laugh. My friend Max came to get his hawk kite.

The Noise

Fred was lying in bed trying to go to sleep. He had a big test the next day. He kept hearing a soft whistle, so he went into the kitchen and checked the tea kettle. The stove was off. Then he stood outside his parents' room to listen for snoring. Everyone was sleeping quietly. He returned to his room and noticed some wind. It wasn't the fan. It was off. He heard a dog bark outside and saw that his window was open a little. He closed it and the noise stopped. He climbed into bed and fell asleep quickly.

The Detectives

It had been raining. Kate and her brother Michael were looking for something entertaining to do. Aunt Sue came into the living room and announced, "I can't find my purse."

The children looked for the missing purse in various parts of the house. Michael looked in the den where his aunt wrote checks, but no purse. Kate searched the bedroom carefully because the purse was last seen there. It wasn't there, but Kate recalled that her aunt had been shopping earlier that day. She ran outside. Just as she arrived, Michael was opening the trunk and Kate saw the purse.

The Strange Gift

Cheryl sat quietly, staring at the tiny black and green slip of paper in her hand. She was remembering how moved she had been when Marlene first gave it to her. Cheryl knew her best friend was poor. Marlene couldn't afford even a small gift for Cheryl's twelfth birthday. She was surprised when Marlene pulled her aside and timidly handed her a pretty, gift-wrapped box with a bow on it. Inside there was a ticket. Cheryl was touched by her friend's gesture. She never imagined that the slip of paper would be the winning ticket for their classroom drawing.

Stranger at Willowbrook

Phil entered Willowbrook School for the first time. The five-minute bell rang. As he hurried to math class, an unfamiliar voice asked, "How's it going, Phil?" Startled, Phil responded with a quick wave and continued on to room 203. During lunch, Phil saw the stranger in the cafeteria, but he pretended not to notice. During the last period, Mr. Nichols was taking attendance when Phil heard a familiar name called. "Zack Wilson," thought Phil. "I remember when we used to build block houses in kindergarten." Phil turned to find Zack and realized that the stranger was a forgotten friend.

Black Out

The soft buzz of the computer relaxed
Anthony as he worked on his yearly report
for his anxious employer. He typed the
final sentence, sighed in relief, and saved
the computer file. The office lights
flickered, the computer screen went black,
and New York City was silent. Sirens
sounded in the area. Flashlights guided the
impatient crowd to sunlight twenty floors
down. An hour later, the police chief
announced through his loud speaker, "All
is clear." The workers filed into the
elevators like clockwork, returning to their
projects. One observer commented, "All
in a day's work in New York City."

Sunset

Alix was enjoying the sunset from Daisy Hill. The magnificent display of bright orange, red, and yellow appeared to be a sweet, ripe mango slowly sinking into the earth. Alix was again surrounded by the beautiful colors of falling leaves as she reluctantly headed home for dinner. Turning east toward the house, she witnessed a horrible sight; her greenhouse was enveloped in flames! She quickly dashed down the hill and across a field of drying corn stalks. A few yards before she arrived, she realized the fire was only a reflection of the sunset on the glass of the greenhouse.

Form

Graded Word Lists

List CC	**List C**
1. see	1. red
2. you	2. day
3. school	3. in
4. to	4. for
5. can	5. have
6. good	6. walk
7. soon	7. boy
8. into	8. cake
9. up	9. your
10. big	10. again
11. man	11. bee
12. look	12. come
13. away	13. picture
14. stop	14. said
15. that	15. put
16. yard	16. word
17. train	17. baby
18. truck	18. car
19. black	19. no
20. white	20. funny

List C 7141

1. ball
2. new
3. fast
4. has
5. with
6. children
7. work
8. pet
9. ready
10. much
11. came
12. parade
13. hen
14. live
15. hear
16. far
17. thing
18. year
19. hurry
20. met

List C 8224

1. brave
2. top
3. it's
4. follow
5. gold
6. front
7. family
8. knock
9. count
10. smell
11. afraid
12. done
13. silver
14. face
15. visit
16. mountain
17. track
18. pile
19. been
20. through

List C 3183

1. pack
2. matter
3. hang
4. center
5. chew
6. rule
7. pound
8. danger
9. force
10. history
11. spend
12. wisdom
13. mind
14. adventure
15. mental
16. harbor
17. fault
18. pilot
19. usually
20. though

List C 5414

1. thunder
2. friendship
3. crickets
4. yesterday
5. dozen
6. telescope
7. whiskers
8. skunk
9. amount
10. nature
11. level
12. husky
13. sight
14. distance
15. hunger
16. figure
17. medicine
18. ashamed
19. saddle
20. anxious

COPY

List C 8595

1. brag

2. college

3. tend

4. ditch

5. bully

6. journal

7. public

8. goblin

9. ransom

10. remarkable

11. ankle

12. social

13. gym

14. education

15. darling

16. muscle

17. pouch

18. barley

19. petticoat

20. invitation

List C 6867

1. youngster

2. activity

3. research

4. grizzly

5. tornado

6. ruffle

7. judgment

8. nylon

9. fable

10. exact

11. decay

12. substitute

13. wealthy

14. communicate

15. assemble

16. economics

17. biscuit

18. forbid

19. attractive

20. pliers

List C 3717

1. jazz
2. puncture
3. fantastic
4. publication
5. derby
6. terminal
7. hemisphere
8. paralyze
9. environment
10. cantaloupe
11. blockade
12. ornamental
13. warrant
14. bombard
15. typhoon
16. hypnotize
17. browse
18. nasal
19. tuberculosis
20. lacquer

List C 8183

1. motive
2. function
3. transplant
4. impressive
5. encircle
6. linoleum
7. investment
8. fortify
9. maximum
10. detain
11. leaflet
12. privacy
13. lubricant
14. oblong
15. liberal
16. identification
17. energetic
18. carburetor
19. antiseptic
20. infuriate

List C 4959

1. nationality
2. complex
3. bleach
4. comparable
5. overwhelm
6. contraction
7. equivalent
8. conservative
9. bewitch
10. insignificant
11. earthy
12. monogram
13. redeem
14. amputate
15. disastrous
16. disband
17. coronation
18. barracks
19. abolition
20. vestibule

List C 1047

1. organism
2. tart
3. ashtray
4. consultant
5. intolerable
6. synthetic
7. conclusive
8. diverse
9. premature
10. insufferable
11. cater
12. reformatory
13. demolition
14. disintegrate
15. hoax
16. granulate
17. necessitate
18. illegitimate
19. gaseous
20. revue

List C 1187

1. nonexistent
2. recession
3. prohibition
4. collaborate
5. philosophy
6. franchise
7. essence
8. flagrant
9. replenish
10. anesthetic
11. monotone
12. instigate
13. cataract
14. sedative
15. memoir
16. dubious
17. premonition
18. libel
19. maladjustment
20. claimant

List C 1296

1. fusion
2. modulate
3. infectious
4. delusion
5. marginal
6. vulnerable
7. inalienable
8. fiscal
9. convene
10. avid
11. platitude
12. predecessor
13. amity
14. detonate
15. caste
16. atrophy
17. amenable
18. omnibus
19. arable
20. meritorious

Form

Graded Passages

Apples

I like apples.

I like red and yellow apples.

Apples can be green.

I like to eat big apples.

An apple is a fun snack.

Fun

"Here it comes!" said Tom.

"I can see it," said Dan. "Here comes the band!"

Tom jumped up and down. "Look at the man. He is tall. I can see his red hat."

"Look!" said Dan. "I see a dog. The dog is big. The dog is brown and white."

Food for Birds

"See the small birds," said Jim. "They are looking in the snow. They want food."

"The snow is deep," said Sue. "They cannot find food."

Jim said, "Let's help them."
"Yes," said Sue. "We can get bread for them."

Jim and Sue ran home. They asked Mother for bread. Mother gave bread to them. Then they ran to find the birds.

"There are the birds," said Sue. "Give them the bread."
Jim put the bread on the snow.
Sue said, "Look at the birds! They are eating the bread."

"They are happy now," said Jim. "They are fat and happy."

Fun with Leaves

Bill had many leaves in his yard. He raked them into a big pile. Pat helped.

Then Bill got a very good idea. He ran and jumped in that pile of leaves.

"Wow! What fun!"
"Let me jump," said Pat. He jumped in the leaves.

Soon both boys were jumping. They threw leaves up into the air.

Mother looked out and said, "I see two boys having fun. Come in for something to eat."

"See our big pile!" said Bill.
"Where?" asked Mother.

The boys looked around. The pile was not big now. The leaves were all over the yard.

Zoo Work

Bob works at the zoo. He takes care of all kinds of animals. The animals are brought to the zoo from all over the world. Bob gives hay to the elephants. He feeds raw meat to the lions and fresh fish to the seals. He knows just what to give every animal. Each day Bob washes the cages in the zoo. When an animal gets sick, Bob takes it to the zoo doctor. He will make it well. Bob keeps the zoo keys. When the people go home, Bob locks the gates to the zoo. Then he can go home.

The Pet Shop

Maria really wanted a little dog. One day she went with her parents to the pet shop. They looked at the fish, turtles, parrots, and many kinds of dogs. Maria and her parents saw one nice puppy that acted very lively. It looked like a small, bouncing, black ball of fur. The puppy was a fluffy black poodle. It jumped around in its cage. When Maria petted the puppy, it sat up and begged. Maria and her parents laughed because the poodle looked so cute. They decided to buy the poodle. After all, who could resist such a cute dog?

The Soccer Game

There were only two minutes to go in the big soccer game between the Jets and the Bombers. The score was tied. The ball was in the Jets' area dangerously close to their goal. Rosa, a Jets midfielder, ran for the ball. She got to the ball and delivered a great kick. The ball went sailing over the midline into Bomber territory.

With a yell, Kim got the ball and dribbled toward the Bomber goal. There was no time for a mistake. The shot must be true. Kim faked right. Then Kim kicked left and scored as the game ended.

Form C • Graded Passage • Student Copy

Pioneer House Building

When the first pioneers came to
America, there were no special people
to build houses, so they did the work
together. All the people in the area
would come and help. Some people
would cut trees. Other people would take
this wood and start forming the frame
of the house. The older children
helped by carting bits of wood or
cutting the limbs. Younger children
played. The work was difficult and
long and gave the people enormous
appetites. Large quantities of food
were prepared and set outside on long
wooden tables. Then everyone gathered
around the table and feasted joyfully.

Museum Visit

On our field trip we visited the new museum. We saw different exhibits about science and the world around us. The telephone exhibit was definitely the most interesting. Phones from the early days were made of wood and metal. People had to ring the operator to make a call. The exhibit displayed many other types of phones. Some had televisions so that you could see the person you were talking to. There were also wireless phones for people and cars that transmit calls through tower signals. We saw movies that showed us how telephones help us in our everyday lives.

Capture and Freedom

One of the most beloved tales is of the princess and a knight. The princess, shackled to a rock, caught the eye of the wandering knight. He galloped over and, with a single stroke of his sword, freed her from the iron chain. Taking her hand, he led her away from the dreadful confinement of the rock. While relaxing in a sunny meadow, he comforted her with reassuring words. The princess told him that she had been seized by pirates. These pirates had brought her to this savage island as a peace offering to the terrible monsters of the sea.

Mount Kilarma

The large mountain loomed ominously in the foreground. Many had tried to defeat this magnificent creation of nature, but to date no one had. There it was, the lonely unconquered giant, Mount Kilarma. In sheer size, there was nothing imposing about the 15,000 foot height of Mount Kilarma. The dangers rested in the skirt of glaciers around the steep sides of the mountain and in the fiercely changing winds that tore at the summit. The small band of mountaineers stared at the huge mass of ice. Could they reach the mountain's peak and do what no one had ever accomplished?

Form D

Graded Passages

Ted's Dog

Ted has a dog.
His name is Ben.
Ben is a big dog.

He can jump up.
Ted pets Ben.
He is a fun dog.

Form D • Graded Passage • Student Copy

COPY

Pete's Red Ball

"I can not find my ball," said Pete. "My ball is a big ball. It is red."

"Here is a ball," Rose said. "The ball is blue. It is little. It is not red."

"I see a ball," said Pete. "It is red. It is big. It is my ball."

Jill's Egg

A white house was in the woods. Jill lived there. The sun made Jill happy. The air smelled clean. She took a walk.

Jill found something along the road in the grass. It was round and white.

"Oh!" said Jill. "What a nice egg. I'll take it home."

Mother was home.

She said, "Jill, you must keep the egg warm."

Jill filled a box with rags. She set the egg in it. She put it near the stove.

The next day Jill heard a sound she did not know.

"Cheep." A baby bird was born. Jill had a new pet.

At the Zoo

Dan wanted to go to the zoo. He
asked his mother. She said, "Yes."
Dan had fun at the zoo. There were many
animals he liked. One animal looked like it
had two tails. It was an elephant. One had
a nice back to ride on. It was a big turtle.
Dan looked at many things. He saw many
furry animals. He laughed at them.

It got dark. "Where is my mother?"
he asked. Dan looked and looked for his
mother. He was lost! He sat down and
cried. Then Dan looked up. He saw
his mother running to him!

A Spider Friend

A spider sat down by a boy. The boy was afraid of it. He should not have been scared. The spider would not hurt him. Most spiders are friendly. Spiders belong to a group of animals that have eight legs. Spiders are not insects.

In the fall the mother spider lays about 500 eggs. Only the strong baby spiders live. When spring comes they leave their nest. They eat flies, bugs, and ants. They also eat insects that harm our crops. Some large spiders eat mice and birds. You should be able to find a spider web where you live.

Cricket Song

It is a summer night. I try to sleep, but a sound keeps waking me. It is a cricket. This bug does not sing with its mouth. The rough wings of the male cricket make sounds. It rubs its wings against each other.

I try to find the bug, but it is hard. The sound does not come from one spot. It would also be hard to see the cricket because it can be as small as the nail on my thumb. Some people think the cricket brings luck. Maybe they know how to fall asleep to the cricket song.

Amazing Plants

There are over three hundred thousand different kinds of plants. The oxygen in the air we breathe comes from plants. Some plants grow bigger and live longer than animals. Plants grow in many sizes and shapes. Some are smaller than the period at the end of this sentence. These plants can only be seen with a microscope. Other plants, like the giant pine, tower high in the sky. Most plants have stems and leaves. Plants can live in a variety of places. Some even seem to grow out of rocks. Others live in water, old bread, and even old shoes!

Flight

Older airplanes were moved through the air by the use of propellers. Now, most planes are driven by large jet engines. Some fly faster than sound. The first thing you may notice about a plane is the wings that stick out on either side of its long body. Today jet planes land and take off from major airports every few seconds. People can travel several hundred miles in less than an hour. It can take travelers longer to retrieve their luggage than to fly to their destination. Planes have been much improved since the Wright brothers first flew in 1903.

Sunflowers

One of the most amazing flowers found in the Midwest is the sunflower. Legend states that the flower got its name from its strange habit of "turning" its head in order to face the sun. The sunflower is a very strong plant. It ranges in height from three to fifteen feet. The head of the sunflower is similar to that of a daisy. Both have an outer circle of wide petals and an inner circle of small brown flowers. Seeds later form from these small flowers. These seeds produce some of the most unique patterns found in the plant world.

Indian Celebrations

Indians worshipped the power in natural things, such as the stars, moon, and the sun. At various times during the year, they would hold celebrations in honor of this power that they named the Great Spirit. On these occasions, they would have ceremonies of dancing and feasting. The Indians would decorate their bodies and faces and dress themselves in their best clothes. A medicine man would lead them in the celebration that continued for several days. While gathered about the council fire, the Indians prayed that the Great Spirit would reveal its wish for them by sending a natural sign.

Our Environment

Besides using plants and animals for food, people use the hides of animals for shoes, the wood from trees to build houses, the fiber from the cotton plant to make skirts and shirts, and the wool from sheep to make suits and coats. Even the synthetic fibers that people use are made from matter found in the environment.

People and the environment are interdependent, but that is not the whole story. Modern people can do much more; they can use science and technology to change their environment. Because of their advanced brains, people can investigate and use their precious environment.

Form E

Graded Passages

A Spider

A spider can be big or little.
It has eight legs.
It has a head and tummy.

It can spin a web. It eats bugs.

The Sun

The sun helps plants grow. The sun makes them green. The sun helps them get food. People eat plants.

The sun helps people. It gives them light. They can see.

The sun helps animals. It helps keep them warm. Some animals eat in the day. It helps them see food.

The Pig Farm

It was hot. Dad and Lisa went to a farm. The farm was a pig farm.

"Look at the pigs!" said Dad.

Lisa said, "I see a pig with white spots. It is white and black."

Dad said, "This one is red."

"Look Lisa," said Dad. "This one has a funny tail."

"The pigs like to play," said Lisa.

Pigs like mud. They play in it. The mud helps keep them cool on hot days.

A farm man talks to us. He says pigs cannot see well. But pigs have good noses.

Lisa said, "My nose helps me find pigs."

The Moon

The moon has a face. My friend says it is a man. I asked Miss Green. She said the moon face was made by big rocks that bumped and bumped. This made big holes. At night the holes look like a face. No one lives on the moon. It is too hot or cold to live there. It is hard to walk on the moon, too. I would be too light. I would go up into the sky.

The moon seems to change from big to little and back again. I like to see it before I go to sleep.

Colors and Light

The sky is blue and the grass is green. Colors help make the world beautiful. Light helps us see colors. You may have seen water waves while swimming. Light makes waves that we cannot see. Different parts of the waves make different colors.

Sometimes the sun shines when it is raining and makes a rainbow. The rain bends the light from the sun. You can see red, orange, yellow, green, blue, and purple at the same time. You can make a rainbow. On a sunny day, spray water into the air. Look closely and you may see a nice rainbow.

NECCO Wafers

NECCO (Neck-o) Wafers have been eaten by children for over 150 years. They come in eight flavors and colors. The pink ones spark in the dark when broken in dry places. People all over the world like to eat them. In 1913, they were taken to the North Pole. Explorers brought them to eat and give to children. They went to the South Pole in 1930. Enough were taken for each person to eat a pound a week for two years! Today, 120 wafers will be eaten each second. This year enough wafers will be sold to circle the world twice.

Bubbles

Soap bubbles can be fun to play with on a hot
summer day. Dip your wand in the bottle and blow
gently or spin around quickly. This is just one kind
of bubble. You may have seen other forms too.
Large boxes may have plastic bubble wrap to
help keep the objects inside from breaking. These
bubbles are fun to pop. Another kind of bubble can
be found in soda or pop. It is made when carbonated
water is mixed with sugar and flavors. When you
blow into a straw that is in soda, the forced air
forms many bubbles.

Seaweed

Some of the oldest plants in the world can be found in the ocean. They are called algae or seaweed. Brown seaweed or kelp can be found in cold water. It contains a high amount of iodine. This seaweed is used to make jelly and make-up. Red seaweed is mostly found in the lower parts of the ocean. It has no roots, but uses hold-fasts to hold to the bottom of the ocean floor. Sometimes red seaweed is fed to cattle because of its nutritious value. Green algae lives in fresh water. One-celled forms of this seaweed can swim.

Cave Icicles

It is common to see icicles formed when water drips off house roofs during winter time in cold climates. The same process slowed down helps explain how stone icicles form in caves. Water dripping from the ceiling of a cave contains a mineral called calcite, and pieces sometimes stick to the ceiling. The water can also carry calcite to the floor. After several years, a small stone icicle slowly begins to form. They build less than an inch per year. Many do not get any longer than one foot. Colored icicles are created when the water contains iron or copper.

The Cornet

Over 300 years ago in Germany, a trumpet called the cornet was very popular. It was considered to be one of the most difficult wind instruments to play. The cornet is made from a curved piece of wood which is carved to make eight sides and then wrapped in leather. Six holes and one thumbhole are covered by different fingers to sound notes, just like a recorder. The mouthpiece is a metal or ivory cup that can be removed until the musician is ready to blow into the instrument. Cornets still exist, but they are usually straight instead of curved.

Sailing Explorers

Over 300 years ago, many English and Dutch companies hired sailors to find new water routes so they could claim land and trade goods more easily. An English company employed Henry Hudson, an English sea captain. The goal was to find a northeast passage between Europe and Asia. After many attempts blocked by polar ice, he was hired by the Dutch East India Trade Company. Hudson and his crew began sailing northeast from Europe toward Asia. Hudson then changed course toward the east coast of what is now called the United States, sailing up the Hudson River in New York.

Graded Passages

A Day in the Woods

Sue was visiting her grandparents' farm for a week. She decided to have a picnic in the woods. She packed a lunch with a peanut-butter and jelly sandwich, an apple, two cookies, and grape juice to drink. Sue had put her lunch in her backpack and started out the door when she remembered Jane. She ran back into the house and got Jane, her favorite doll.

Sue had a good time in the woods. She walked on small paths that the animals had made. After walking all morning, she was very hungry. At noon she found a fallen tree and sat on it to eat her lunch.

After lunch Sue found an animal trail that led to a quiet spring. She looked into the water and saw small fish swimming. She must remember to tell her grandparents about the little fish in the spring.

Sue realized that it was time to start back to her grandparents' house, but she didn't know which way to go. Just then she heard rustling in the bushes right behind her. She was frightened and started to run. The noise followed her as she ran. It kept getting closer. All of a sudden something jumped at her! It was Rusty, her grandparents' dog. Sue was so happy to see him she gave him a big hug.

Sue and Rusty returned to the farm just as the sun was setting. Sue's grandparents were worried. Sue promised never to go so deep in the woods again.

Danny and the Dragon

"Mother, there's a dragon after me! It won't go away!"

The next day when Danny went out, there it was. It roared and blew fire at Danny. It was so big and Danny was so small. "Leave me alone!"

Danny ran down the path to the river and hid behind a rock to see if the dragon was still coming. It was. He had to get rid of that dragon. He went home through the woods. He needed a plan to trick the dragon.

In bed that night, Danny made his plan. He had to trick the dragon into the river. He knew the dragon couldn't swim.

While it was still dark, Danny climbed out his window. He got a rope and tiptoed away from his house. Then he ran to the big rock by the river. Danny laid the rope across the path. He tied one end of the rope to a tree. He laid the other end on the ground behind the big rock. Danny ran home through the woods. There was the dragon lying by the door to his house. Danny climbed quietly in his window to wait.

In the morning Danny went out. Roaring, the dragon blew fire and leaped at him. Danny dodged it and ran toward the river. He flew down the path, dove behind the rock, and grabbed the rope.

Down the path came the dragon. Then it tripped on the rope and crashed into the river. The river carried it far, far away.

I Want to Fly

Jerry, looking at the sky, promised himself, "I'm going to fly some day."

Jerry, a ten-year-old boy from a small town in Iowa, had dreamed of flying since he was a little boy. He wasn't just going to fly in an airplane. He was going to fly like a hawk.

He spent many hours watching hawks fly. They made it look so easy. With their powerful wings they built up speed, then they would glide. It was beautiful and breath-taking watching them ride the air currents. "I am going to fly."

As he climbed to the top of the cliff, his imagination was far ahead of him telling him how exciting it would be. At the top he paused only for a moment; then he dove off the cliff into the air. "This is wonderful! This is better than I had ever imagined!" He soared, he dipped, and rose again, riding the air currents. Flying was better than he had imagined.

When Jerry awoke, his parents were standing by the hospital bed. "The doctor said you will be fine. You will have to miss two more weeks of school because of your tonsil operation."

After Jerry's parents left, he thought a moment, "I really felt like I was flying. I could feel the cool air blowing through my hair. I saw the landscape below me." Was it a dream or not? If it was a dream, where did he get the brownish hawk feather he was holding?

Action at Brantwood

As Kay got off the passenger train at Brantwood, she was rudely shoved. Turning quickly, she saw a young man elbowing his way through the bustling crowd toward an older woman. As Kay proceeded across the train platform, she saw the older woman trip and tumble to the pavement. The fallen woman's handbag flew open and its contents spilled all over the ground. Her suitcase also snapped open and its contents, too, were strewn over the snow.

Kay rushed up to help the stunned woman. She was brushed aside by the man who had collided with her earlier. The man assumed charge of the woman's belongings in a most possessive manner. He was short, slender, blonde, and had a rosy complexion. Kay picked up the woman's handbag from the snow, but the young man snatched it from her almost as if he suspected her of trying to steal it.

"Just a minute, please!" exclaimed Kay. "I'm just trying to help this lady. May I ask why you are trying to take charge of her things?"

"I am her son!" retorted the young man unpleasantly as he went on hastily collecting the things which had burst from the suitcase. Kay concentrated her attention on the woman and tried to help her up. "Where are my purse and my suitcase!" she cried anxiously.

"Your son has them," Kay said reassuringly. "Don't worry. He'll bring you everything as soon as he collects it."

"My son!" the lady exclaimed sharply. "I have no son!"

Adapted from *The Double Disguise* by Frances K. Judd.

A sharp sound startled him. Somewhere, off in the blackness, someone had fired a gun three times.

Rainsford sprang up and moved quickly to the rail, mystified. He strained his eyes in the direction from which the reports had come, but it was like trying to see through a blanket. He leaped up onto the rail and balanced himself there to get a greater elevation; his pipe, striking a rope, was knocked from his mouth. He lunged for it. A short, hoarse cry came from his lips as he realized he had reached too far and had fallen overboard. The cry was pinched off as the blood-warm waters of the Caribbean Sea closed over his head.

He struggled up to the surface and tried to cry for help, but the wash from the speeding yacht slapped him in the face. The salty water in his open mouth gagged and strangled him. Desperately he struck out with strong strokes after the receding lights of the yacht, but he stopped before he had covered fifty feet. He calmed down and assessed his situation. It was not the first time he had been in a tough situation. There was a chance that his cries could be heard by someone aboard the yacht. But the chance was slim and grew much slimmer as the yacht continued on. He shouted with all his might. The lights of the yacht became faint, looking like ever-vanishing fireflies. Then they were blotted out entirely by the black night.

Adapted from "The Most Dangerous Game" by Richard Connell. Copyright, 1924, by Richard Connell. Copyright renewed, 1952, by Louise Fox Connell. Special adaptation permission of reprint by Brandt & Brandt Literary Agents, Inc.

The Angel of the Candy Counter

The Angel of the candy counter had found me out at last and was demanding extreme payment for all the Snickers, Mounds, suckers, and Hershey bars. I had two huge cavities that were rotten to the gums. The pain was well past the help of crushed aspirins or oil of cloves. Only one thing could help me now, so I prayed earnestly that I'd be allowed to sit under the house and have the entire building collapse on my jaw.

Since there was no dentist in Stamps, nor doctor either, for that matter, Momma had dealt with other toothaches. She would try yanking them out with a string tied to the tooth and the other end looped over her fist, as well as pain killers and prayer. In this case the medicine proved ineffective. There wasn't enough enamel left to hook a string on, and the prayers were being ignored because some demon was blocking their way.

I lived some days and nights in blinding pain, not so much toying with, as seriously considering, the idea of jumping in the well. So Momma decided I had to be taken to a dentist. The nearest dentist was in Mason, twenty miles away, and I was sure that I'd be dead long before we reached half the distance. Momma said we'd go to Dr. Lincoln, and he'd take care of me. She said we'd have to take the bus. I didn't know of anyone who'd been to see him, but we had to go.

Adapted from *I Know Why the Caged Bird Sings* by Maya Angelou. Reprinted by permission of Random House, Inc.

The Most Beautiful

Of the gods of ancient Greece, Apollo was the most beautiful. His hair was brilliant gold; his eyes were stormy blue. He wore a flowing tunic of golden panther skin, carried a quiver of golden arrows, and used a golden bow. His chariot was beaten gold; his horse was white with a platinum mane and flame-colored eyes. Apollo was always the god of the sun, but later he became patron of music, poetry, mathematics, and medicine. As an adult, Apollo was known for his unparalleled wisdom, but in his youth he was known for his barbarous exploits. Several times he was almost expelled from the company of the gods by Zeus, whom he angered with his youthful folly.

One objectionable folly was Apollo's treatment of a satyr named Marsyas. Marsyas was an excellent musician; Apollo considered this his talent and would allow no rivalry. Hearing Marsyas praised continually, Apollo invited him to a musical contest. The winner was to choose a penalty to which the loser would have to submit, and the Muses were their judges. Marsyas played his melodious flute, and Apollo played his lyre. They played so exquisitely that the Muses could not choose between them, so Apollo suggested that they play their instruments upside down and sing simultaneously. Apollo turned his lyre upside down, played, and chanted a beautiful poem. Because Marsyas could not play his flute upside down and sing at the same time, the despondent satyr was declared the loser. Consequently, Apollo collected the prize.

Adapted from *The Greek Gods* by Bernard Evslin, Dorothy Evslin, and Ned Hoopes. Reprinted by permission of Scholastic Book Services.

Elizabeth Meets Darcy

Elizabeth watched for the first appearance of Pemberley Woods with some perturbation; and when at length they turned in at the lodge, her spirits were in a high flutter.

The park was very large and contained great variety of ground. They entered it in one of its lowest points, and drove for some time through a beautiful wood, stretching over a wide extent.

Elizabeth's mind was too full for conversation, but she saw and admired every remarkable spot and point of view. They gradually ascended for half a mile, and then found themselves at the top of a considerable eminence, where the wood ceased, and the eye was immediately captured by Pemberley House, situated on the opposite side of a valley, into which the road with some abruptness wound. It was a large, handsome, stone structure, standing well on rising ground, and backed by a ridge of high woody hills. She had never seen a place for which nature had enhanced more, or where natural beauty had been so little counteracted by an awkward taste. They were all of them warm in their admiration, and at the moment she felt that to be mistress of Pemberley might be something!

They descended the hill, crossed the bridge, and drove to the door; and, while examining the nearer aspect of the house, all her apprehensions of meeting its owner returned. As she walked across the lawn, Elizabeth turned back to look again, and the owner himself suddenly came forward from the road.

Adapted from *Pride and Prejudice* by Jane Austen.

Bookworm or Earthworm

To read or to weed is the problem that confronts me whenever I have a few spare minutes. Reading satisfies the wanderlust in me. It affords the opportunity to abandon the monotonous ruts of everyday life and to traipse excitedly along the mysterious trails in the enchanting land of books. Lost in the magic of the printed page, I can cast off my customary garments and array myself in the raiment of a victorious knight or a soccer star. No longer shackled by the chains of time and space, I shiver with Washington's valiant men in the piercing cold of Valley Forge and I kneel in reverent awe at Bethlehem's crib. Is it any wonder that I am unable to resist the beckoning call of a good book?

My interest in weeding is probably the result of my interest in reading. This occupation puts me on a par with those noble characters that I have respected in books. Few chores are more intriguing to me than that of rescuing struggling plants from the greedy claws of choking weeds. I like the feel of the cold and damp earth as I eject the intruding roots. With the confident swagger of a conquering hero, I march triumphantly through our flower garden, leaving grateful shrubs in my wake. Even the squirming worms wriggle their gratitude for my noble deed. Yes, recreation time is always debating time for me. The topic of this secret controversy ever remains the same: to read or to weed?

Adapted with permission from *Voyages in English* by Reverend Paul E. Campbell and Sister Mary Donatus Macnickle. Copyrighted by Loyola University Press.

American in Paris

On a brilliant day in May, in the year 1868, a gentleman was reclining at his ease on the great circular divan which occupied the center of the Salon Carré, in the Museum of the Louvre. He had taken serene possession of the softest spot of this commodious ottoman. With his head thrown back and his legs outstretched, he was staring at Murillo's beautiful moon-borne Madonna in profound enjoyment of his posture. He had removed his hat and flung down beside him a little red guidebook and an opera glass. The day was warm; he was heated with walking, and he repeatedly passed his handkerchief over his forehead with a somewhat wearied gesture. His exertions on this particular day had been of an unwonted sort, and he had often performed great physical feats which left him less jaded than his tranquil stroll through the Louvre. He had looked at all the pictures to which an asterisk was affixed in those formidable pages of fine print in his Bädeker guidebook; his attention had been strained and his eyes dazzled, and he had sat down with an aesthetic headache. His physiognomy would have sufficiently indicated that he was a shrewd and capable fellow. In truth, he had often sat up all night over a bristling bundle of accounts and heard the cock crow without a yawn. But Raphael and Titian and Rubens were a new kind of arithmetic, and they made him, for the first time in his life, really wonder.

Adapted from *The American* by Henry James.

Graded Passages

Hawks

Most hawks hunt for prey alone. In New Mexico, there is a type of hawk called Harris' hawks. Harris' hawks work together as a team to catch their prey. This idea was interesting to a wildlife scientist. He decided to study these hawks.

The first thing he had to do was catch one hawk in a group. He then put a radio transmitter on the bird's leg. This helped him keep track of where the bird went. He did this with one hawk from each group.

The scientist went to a high place to watch the hawks. This took a lot of time and hard work. He discovered that most of the time the hawks caught rabbits. These were large rabbits that would be hard for one hawk to catch. The hawks worked together as a team so that they could catch their prey. Then they all shared the meal.

The scientist watched as the hawks would stalk their prey. First, they would fly across a large area. Sometimes the hawks would sit in trees to watch the ground. When the hawks saw a rabbit, they would start following it. When the rabbit slowed down in an open place, the hawks would dive at it. The hawks would wait until the rabbit became tired to make their final dive.

These hawks are very good at working as a team. This helps them to find food and stay alive. They have learned that it is very important to help each other.

It was early winter when Martha and Johnny Stine began their journey. They were traveling from Kansas to Colorado. When it was night, they would set up camp wherever they could. This type of trip was not easy. The year was 1891, which was before cars or airplanes. Good roads were not available. Martha and Johnny traveled in a covered wagon pulled by horses.

As time passed, the weather became colder. One night when they stopped to sleep, it was six degrees below zero. The next night they were caught in a blizzard. Martha and Johnny stopped at a house to ask for directions. They were asked if they wanted to spend the night there because of the blizzard. Johnny didn't want to stay, although Martha did. They continued on their journey in the blinding blizzard until they could no longer see. The roads were covered with snow. The team of horses couldn't be forced to continue through the ice and snow any longer. Then they saw the shadow of a small cabin. When they reached the cabin, it was locked. They pulled up beside the cabin in order to get shelter from the wind and snow. Weary, they fell into a restless sleep. Martha felt very depressed. They were lost in a blizzard and tired from traveling.

Four days later they arrived at their destination. Martha was so happy she cried. It had been four long weeks since they had started. Martha was happy to see the trip end.

Orville and Wilbur Wright invented and built the first successful airplane. Orville flew it in December of 1903. These famous brothers had an interesting childhood.

In 1879, Wilbur was twelve and Orville was eight. Their father brought them a toy made of paper, bamboo sticks, and cork after a trip to Ohio. It was called a helicopter. They turned a stick that twisted a rubber band, fastened it, and then tossed the helicopter into the air. Orville and Wilbur reached to catch it before it fell. The toy helicopter flew several feet across the room. The boys played with it until it broke.

Orville had many plans for making money. He learned to make and fly kites, and he made money by selling them to his friends. By the time he was fourteen, he had a printing press and business. Wilbur became interested in the business. In a short time, they published a weekly newspaper.

Bicycles became popular in the 1890s. These early bikes were very dangerous and difficult to ride. The front wheel was five feet high. The back wheel was eighteen inches high. A new bicycle was then built with two wheels of equal size, similar to today's bikes. The brothers rented a shop. They began repairing and selling bicycles. Now they had two businesses.

One day, Wilbur saw a photograph of a glider with a man hanging beneath the wings. He showed it to Orville. That may have been the beginning of their serious talk of flying.

Teacher

Many people know that Helen Keller was deaf and blind. Not as many people know about Anne Sullivan. She taught Helen Keller to read and write and was her companion for fifty years.

Anne Sullivan was born in 1866—more than 135 years ago. She was nearly blind herself. At the age of ten, she was sent to a poor house away from her family. When Anne was fourteen, she was admitted to an institute for the blind in the city of Boston. She had several eye operations and was able to learn to read.

When she was twenty-one, Anne was hired to teach Helen Keller, a seven year old who was deaf and blind. Anne studied how she might teach Helen Keller. In March of 1887, Anne went to Alabama to begin her new job. She even took a doll for Helen.

Teaching Helen was not easy. Anne tried to spell out words on Helen's hand through touch. Once Helen understood, she was able to learn many words. When Helen wanted to know Anne's name, she spelled teacher in Helen's hand. From that day on, Helen called Anne teacher. Anne was also called a miracle worker.

Anne was Helen's teacher and friend for about fifty years. Near the end of Anne's life, her eyesight became very poor again. She went blind. Fortunately, Anne knew all of the letters in braille—an alphabet that makes it possible for blind people to read. When Anne died, she was called truly great.

Have You Played This Game?

You might be one of about 500 million people who have played the best-selling board game in the world. It is sold in 80 countries and offered in 26 languages. Over 200 million games have sold in the world. Say "Monopoly" and people of every age can remember lively games with friends and family. How did this wonder start?

Charles B. Darrow, like most Americans, could not find a job during the Great Depression. At night he started drawing a game board on his kitchen table cloth. Soon he made rules, property cards, and little houses and hotels. Evenings soon found Darrow with friends and family playing his new game. News of the games passed by word of mouth. People asked Darrow for their own sets. Darrow happily made games for his friends. He sensed that his game could become a job.

In 1934, Darrow took Monopoly to executives at Parker Brothers. They dismissed it for 52 design mistakes, but Darrow knew he had a winning game. With help from a friend, he made sets by hand. These sold at a Philadelphia department store. People loved the game and orders soon started flooding in. Darrow knew he couldn't keep up the pace. He went to Parker Brothers a second time. This time they accepted the game and quickly began mass production. That first year, 1935, Monopoly was the best-selling game in America. Monopoly made Darrow the first million-aire game designer, freeing him from ever worrying about a job again.

Friend of Lions

At the break of dawn, he rises from the bed that is placed just outside the door to his hut. Dressed only in shorts and sandals, he sets out on his daily prowl of Kenya's Kora Game Preserve in Eastern Africa. He is looking for lions.

George Adamson is not a hunter; on the contrary, his days are spent trying to preserve what few wild lions remain on this part of the African continent. The Kenyan government closed Adamson's lion rehabilitation program after several people at his camp were assaulted by the cats he considers the perfection of ageless beauty and grace. Now he searches for the lions he returned from captivity and for their offspring. They come to him when he calls. He feeds them like pets, and he protects them from poachers.

In the late 1950s, when he was a government game warden, Adamson shot a man-eating lioness who had a cub. The story of how he and his wife Joy raised the cub, Elsa, is told in the book and the movie titled *Born Free*. This story brought the cause of wildlife conservation to the attention of people in many countries around the world. It also raised $600,000 that has been used for a variety of wildlife conservation projects.

Since Joy's death in 1980, Adamson has wandered the lonely landscape of this vast preserve. His long, flowing, golden hair and white beard make him appear like one of the creatures he loves so much—the lion.

Destruction

Pompeii, an ancient city in Southern Italy, was settled in the 8th century B.C. It was overtaken by the Romans in 310 B.C. and became part of the Roman Empire. During its first five hundred years, Pompeii grew from a small farming village to an important trading center. Then in 62 A.D. an earthquake hit the city, leaving it destroyed. The residents of the city began rebuilding, but while they were in the middle of rebuilding the city temple, a more lasting disaster arrived. Mount Vesuvius, a volcano which had been thought extinct, erupted in 79 A.D. covering Pompeii with hot lava.

Eye-witnesses watched Mount Vesuvius erupt as bright flames towered in the sky and black smoke covered the sun. Volcanic ash and lava covered the city until almost no buildings were left standing. As the volcanic eruption hit Pompeii, the universe seemed to fight against the city sending lightning, earthquakes, and tidal waves. This attack lasted for three days, killing all who had survived the volcano. When the dust settled, 15 feet of smoking debris covered what had once been Pompeii.

Pompeii was buried under ashes, stone, and cinders for almost 2,000 years. After the volcano, looters took what they could find from the city, and Pompeii was forgotten until the nineteenth century when the site was rediscovered and excavation began. Much has been learned about the manners and customs of the ancient Romans. Today, visitors can walk through Pompeii and view a city almost 3,000 years old.

Earthquakes

Earthquakes can be devastating natural disasters. The infamous San Francisco earthquake of 1906 caused over $200-million worth of damage, destroyed almost 30,000 buildings, and killed about 450 persons. In Japan, the cities of Tokyo and Yokohama were leveled by the earthquake of 1923 in which more than 140,000 persons were killed by falling buildings and fires, and over a million people were left homeless—all in 30 seconds.

Hundreds of earthquakes occur every year throughout the world. Fortunately, few are as destructive as those described above. The development of an accurate system for predicting earthquakes would lessen the loss of life and property, but at present scientists can only study these phenomena. The study of earthquakes is called seismology. Seismographs, instruments sensitive to ground movement, are used to chart each motion, and the Richter Scale is commonly used to grade each earthquake's strength on a 1-to-10 scale.

It is now known that earthquakes are created by sudden shifts that occur along faults deep in the earth's crust. According to the Theory of Continental Drift, the earth's crust consists of about twenty rigid sections, or plates, that are in continuous movement. This movement grinds and presses rocks at the edge of the plates. If the pressure becomes too great, the rocks shift, and the resulting movement sends energy, or seismic waves, to the surface of the earth. Most major earthquakes occur along the edge of the plates, and the most damaging impact occurs at the first surface-point reached by the seismic waves.

Beating the Bonk

Bonk describes the symptoms that occur when your body's carbohydrate stores are used up as a result of sustained exercise. As you exercise, most of the fuel being burned is consumed by your muscles. Both fats and carbohydrates can be used for this process. Fat, stored in fatty tissue, is reduced to free fatty acids which are transported by the blood to the muscles. In contrast, carbohydrates are stored within the muscles as glycogen. During exercise, individual molecules of glycogen are removed and used as energy.

Your vital organs also need a continuous supply of fuel. Whether at rest or during exercise, your brain and nervous system depend on blood glucose. The reason why they need glycogen is because the cells of your nervous system don't store glycogen and can't use fat. To meet energy requirements, your blood glucose levels must stay at the same level. This job is largely done by your liver, which contains large amounts of glycogen that can be converted to glucose.

With the muscles and organs vying for glucose, lengthy exercise can drain the liver. When blood glucose levels become too low to meet the fuel requirement of your central nervous system, you begin to feel tired, irritated, and unhappy. In a word, you bonk.

Fortunately, you can remedy the bonk. When your blood glucose levels fall, you can replenish them by eating or drinking something rich in carbohydrates. Carbohydrates are quickly digested into glycogen, which is transported to the liver, muscles, and other organs.

Adapted from *Nutrition for Cyclists*. Rodale Press.

Form LE • Graded Passage • Student Copy

Beards

The history of beards has been a topic of increasing curiosity in today's society. Early man first cherished a beard for religious reasons; primitive races were convinced there was a sacred connection between all parts of a man's body, including his hair, and his personality. Hence, hair had to be carefully guarded from possible foes—this accounts for ancient man's custom of burning hair clippings to prevent them from being used by his enemies for nefarious purposes.

Thus, the earliest beard was faith-conditioned and therefore meticulously cared for. Ancient Egyptians used tongs, curling irons, dyes, and even gold dust to give it a golden sheen.

In those days, shaving was considered perverted. It was a practice reserved for the defeated adversary and the dangerously diseased; lepers were shaved to warn others of their infection. Sometimes those in mourning also shaved as a symbol of vital sacrifice to the dead.

The whims of individual rulers contributed to in determining the fate of beards. For example, Queen Elizabeth I, who disliked beards, taxed anyone sprouting a beard of more than two weeks' growth—the amount of assessment depended upon the man's social standing. In France, the beard became fashionable when it was the personal preference of the current king. Francis I grew a beard to hide an ugly scar on his chin, and his male subjects emulated the fashion. During the eighteenth century, the Spaniards considered the beard to be in poor taste because their king was unable to grow one.

Adapted with permission from *How Did It Begin?* by R. Brasch.

Early Literacy Assessments

O H S E G P

X V I M J D K

B T R Z F N

Y Q W C U A L

b x e c j m g

l u r t q h y

s d o a k w a

i p v f n z g

Alphabet Knowledge • Student Copy

Wordless Picture Reading • Student Copy

1

The cat sits.

2

The cat walks.

3

The cat eats.

4

The cat sleeps.

1. the
2. of
3. and
4. to
5. a
6. in
7. is
8. that
9. it
10. was
11. for
12. you
13. he
14. on
15. as
16. are
17. they
18. with
19. be
20. at

The Cat

Pat has a cat.

The cat is big.

The cat is black.

Pat pets the cat.

The cat likes Pat.

The Red Hen

The red hen sat on a nest.

She had six eggs in the nest.

She did not get up.

She just sat on the eggs.

Graded Passage • Student Copy

Extra Passages

Tom's Day

Today was Tom's birthday. This was supposed to be a special day. Instead, it was a very bad day. He was going to have a birthday party, but his mom was out of town. Jeff, his best friend, had forgotten his birthday. Besides, it was raining. "What a gloomy day," Tom said as he jammed his cold hands into his pockets. He shuffled slowly down the street kicking a stone.

He unlocked the back door and opened it. Wham! He was knocked over by Rusty. Rusty barked and greeted him with a wet lick. As Tom got to his feet, everyone shouted, "Surprise!"

The Astonished Students

There was once a student in Germany named Kristof who thought he could do anything he wanted to do. He was very courageous. One Friday, he coaxed his friend Petra to go in the dark forest. They would build a bonfire. She took the invitation, but was scared. She had heard the legend of the "Furious Scientist." He appeared with the mist of the night. Petra and Kristof went into the forest. The horizon was getting dark. They hiked for ten minutes. Suddenly, both of them left. They were frantically holding their heads talking about a horrifying mist they saw.

New Shoes

Note: Remove the following *New Shoes* booklet for use with the Literacy Knowledge assessment. Bind the booklet on the left side.

New Shoes

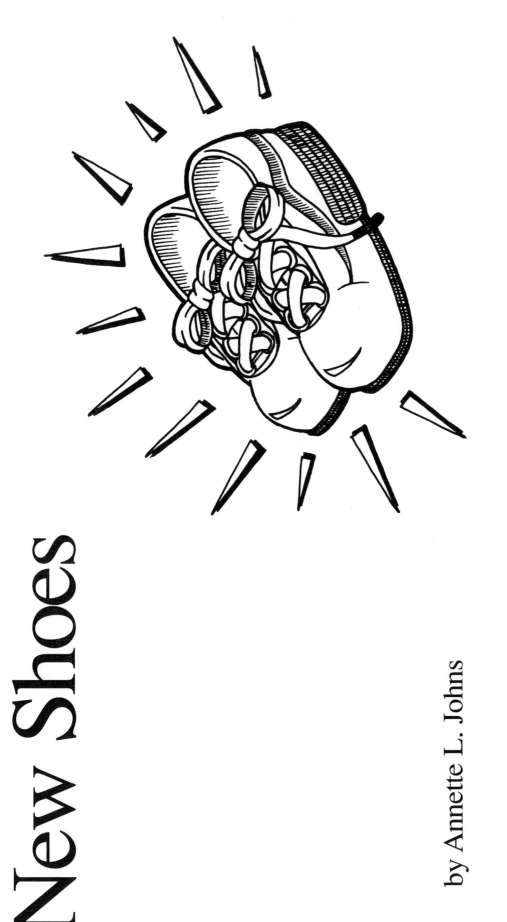

by Annette L. Johns

These are

my shoes.

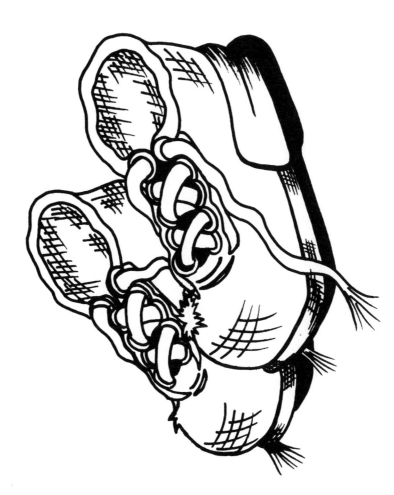

They are getting tight.

They are old.

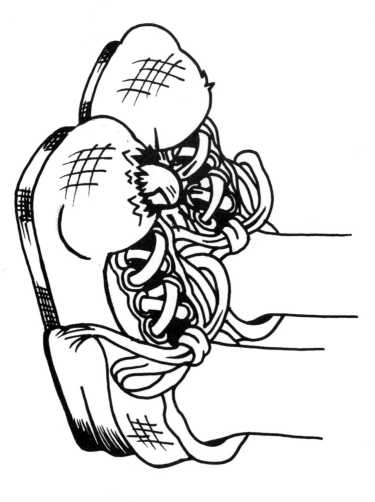

Mommy says,

"It's time for

new shoes."

We go

to the shoe

store.

These shoes

fit me!

Will Mommy buy

these shoes for

me?

Yes!

She pays for them.

6

I am wearing my
new shoes home.

I like my new shoes.

They feel good.

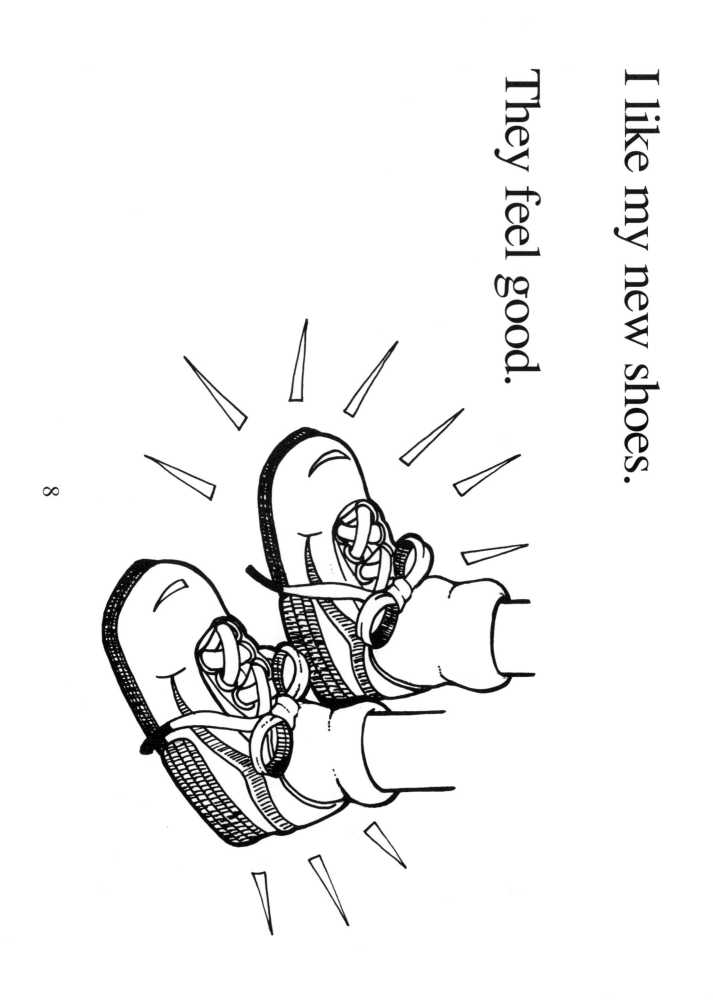

Old shoes are nice, too.

Will Mommy let me keep them?

What do you think?

I think she will.

10

Tabs for Student Booklet

The tabs provided may be reproduced on card stock, cut out and placed on pages in the Student Booklet.

cut here →

Form A	Form B	Form C	Form D
Form E	Form LN	Form LE	Early Literacy Assessment
Extra Passages			

cut here →